Any Given Day

Alabama Poetry Series

General Editors: Dara Wier and Thomas Rabbitt

In the Fourth World, by Sandra M. Gilbert
The Story They Told Us of Light, by Rodney Jones
The Middle of the Journey, by Brian Swann
Memling's Veil, by Mary Ruefle
Fields of Vision, by Mariève Rugo
A Belfry of Knees, by Alberta Turner
The Arctic Herd, by John Morgan
The Invention of Kindness, by Lee Upton
Any Given Day, by Ralph Burns
Esperanza's Hair, by Peggy Shumaker

RALPH BURNS

Any Given Day

The University of Alabama Press

Copyright © 1985 by
The University of Alabama Press
University, Alabama 35486
All rights reserved
Manufactured in the United States of America

Photograph on title page: "Goat Ears" by Roger Pfingston.

Library of Congress Cataloging in Publication Data

Burns, Ralph, 1949–
   Any given day.

   (Alabama poetry series)
   I. Title.   II. Series.
PS3552.U732493A82   1985   811'.54   84-16230
ISBN 0-8173-0259-X
ISBN 0-8173-0260-3 (pbk.)

The epigraph to Part One is from *Selected Poems of Rainer Maria Rilke,*
ed. and trans. by Robert Bly, copyright © 1981 by Harper & Row. Used
by permission.

Josephine Jacobsen's line of poetry on page 40 is from "The Chinese
Insomniacs," © 1978 by The New Yorker Magazine, Inc. The poem later
appeared in *The Chinese Insomniacs,* published in 1981 by the University of
Pennsylvania Press. Used by permission.

"Tall Tale" and "The Barrens of Washington County" were first
published in *College English*. Reprinted by permission of National Council
of Teachers of English.

"Like a Voice behind a Voice" appeared in *Field, #*29, fall 1983, under
U.S. copyright # TX-1-306-596.

for Gladys Dowd Burns

ACKNOWLEDGMENTS

Some of these poems have appeared in the following magazines, to which grateful acknowledgment is made.

College English: "Tall Tale," "The Barrens of Washington County"
Field: "Like a Voice behind a Voice"
Indiana Review: "The Subnormal Girl with a Cat"
The Kenyon Review: "The Jay," "Lacking Sympathy"
Milkweed Chronicle: "Windy Tuesday Nights," "Again, Father"
The Ohio Review: "Joey"
Porch: "Auction," "School Dream"
The Midwest Quarterly: "The Shetland Islands," "The Gift," "The Big Money," "Remembering My Father," "December Twentieth," "Shock Treatment," "March 14–20, 1982, Year of the Eagle," "The House for Sale across the Street"

A few of these poems appeared in WINDY TUESDAY NIGHTS, a chapbook published by Milkweed Editions, an imprint of *Milkweed Chronicle*.

Thanks to the National Endowment for the Arts for a grant during the writing of some of these poems.

Contents

Part One:
The Rich and the Lucky

It's okay for the rich and the lucky to keep still;
no one wants to know about them anyway.
But those in need have to step forward,
have to say: I am blind,
or: I'm about to go blind,
or: nothing is going well with me,
or: I have a child who is sick,
or: right there I'm sort of glued together. . . .

And probably that doesn't do anything either.
—from Rainer Maria Rilke's
"Title Poem" to *The Voices*,
translated by Robert Bly

Again, Father

You are like the man who drove off a dirt road
one Saturday and sat until help came
but the stars only turned over and over
and a family turned their lights on.
You think this story goes on and on,
a tiny contrite scene that passes breath
to solitary breath, wind and stars to
reasonable sky. An old coach said you never
really break your arm but repair it through
memory, you drop your head and close your
eyes and reconcile all loss. Roads I remember
aren't roads anymore. I see them everywhere gone
all those quiet detonative years,
all that summer when your mind went wrong.

Lacking Sympathy

My father fishes the red sun down,
October, a kind of concurrent posture,
a live oak living where it likes
and falling for no reason. Over the pond
the geese form a vee
so he flycasts toward that victory
water lets him have. And here I
am hiding in the trees which
are not trees really but geometric
shapes that say their names grandly.
See? I can't possibly know him.
I can't possibly know his hardship.
One can move I know and not move
like fog. One can be on the earth that is seeming
only incidental. But now as the mourners
pass from house to house and park
their cars on the gravel drive,
I'd place myself above the plum-colored earth
strangely happy. Mine, after all,
are dead or nearly dead. The rooms
we've shared are blind, even now,
you can almost see them watching.
They are practicing to be rooms forever.
You can almost walk in.

Like a Voice behind a Voice

I asked her what's wrong.
She said I don't know, I just
feel strange, and another said she's
probably hallucinating.

I work at this hospital twice a week
and I know the wrong things that
follow a simple conversation.
Some people feel the crush of space,

of things falling from space,
a piece of equipment, a meteor.
Maybe if you stood up I said.
Maybe if you went for a walk.

Outside I hear the sound of a metal bat,
I see the ball that never leaves the air.
It climbs over trees and meadows,
hills and factories, power lines and stacks.

I feel something in my hair,
she said, all tangled. Now
the sun and moon have traded
places. I can hear

the neurasthenic thrush,
the pedantic robin—
I can still hear the sound
she made when a bus backfired.

And Leave Show Business?

This elephant keeper shoved a hose up
the ass of an elephant every day. He
told a man. The man said, *So why don't*
you quit? And the keeper said, *You have*
to understand: elephant bowels are fragile,
you only spray a little and shit flies
all over. . . . And the man said, *I understand,*
I think, someone has to, but why don't you
quit? And the keeper said, *And leave show*
business? I don't know who first told me,
You'll die someday, you can't live forever.
I don't know who took my hand and said,
Some things, not all things, are possible.
At a state mental hospital where I work
I asked a patient once what he remembered.
Everything. Everything that ever happened.
Thinking back, incompletely, I think
I must've disbelieved his ease, his willingness
to witness all his loss always, so I asked,
just having heard the stupid elephant joke:
Anything about elephants? pets? He had a dog:
Bean, Bingo, something like that. And he walked
him every day on a leash and they bought
a hamburger every day on South Harrison
or North Harrison, somewhere in Shelbyville.
I asked where the dog was. He said he loved
him so much he'd drink out of the river
and the dog would too, he loved him
so much. I have to admit I had to say

something and of course there was nothing
to say. His head was down as he drank.
The water was sweet. Easily I left him
alone to walk myself out of the river
of sense. I remember riding shotgun
in a truck with my Uncle Ralph across flat
Kansas. He said something. I said, *Really?*
And he said, *Hell yes boy, do you think
I'd lie? Why do you always say really?*
And I didn't know, God help me, I don't
know. He was my uncle. He wouldn't lie.
Truth is I hadn't been listening,
but watching the long rows pass my window,
I was busy being elephant keeper
and elephant, the hose inside, the dog
that drank with a man, and the river, where
everything is equal, is possible, where
I knew I'd die someday and live without
sight or sound or touch, possibly forever.

I Had No Idea

—beginning with two lines from Bryant Gumbel,
Today Show host, describing a visit by the Queen
of England to the United States

The queen was wearing white chiffon
with orange, California poppies. . . .
This morning I wrestle with
whether the trash men will remove
the cardboard box. For days
you tell me it's more complicated,
that we share the kingdom, we
are members in the same Local.
I'm thinking of balloon frame
construction in housing, the essayist
wrote, how houses fly up and then
the tiny red flags, how a frontier
yawns and we yawn too and sleep
on a bed of silver. Now
it is raining in great pastels,
the rain dissolves the paper
in the street. You didn't tell me
those red things you put in your hair
belong to the river that enjoins
the curb, runs down Sixth,
past the T-Mart and into
the gravel entry at Haag Drugs.
I had not hoped to be so poor.

Joey

Because the plane is almost empty,
about to land, and the lights below,
at the edge of St. Louis, seem a part
made ornamentally whole,
I grip the seat.
Because the idea of flight
belongs to the rich and the lucky,
I'm afraid. I think of Joe Grimaldi, clown.
As a child he was tied and put in a sack
then slung round and round his father's
head by a chain. Once,
when the chain broke,
he landed so softly in the audience
he was invited to the French court
to play the part of a small animal.
That was when Joe learned to be funny.
Right now my friend is almost drunk—
he doesn't believe in Keats,
electric typewriters, ideas, the French.
He's young, I think to myself,
he grew up rich, he's lucky.
He reminds me that the world
falls, that events are chained
only literally, that the plane
could stall and sweep itself out
of the night air and then
where would we be? *I'm Grim all day,*
Joe punned, *but I make you laugh at night.*
I've laughed at anything that makes

me seem better. I should hold the hands
of everyone I've hurt. And I should wait.
As if it takes a good long time
to feel anything and truth is
words can only do so much,
the air is so exaggerated in its wants,
the ground so stubbornly lit.

Then Someone Called, Offering Me a Job

but I don't believe it,
not until I sign something
and witness the same document being signed
by the appropriate official,
and then not until we rent the U-Haul
and our sweet friends see us off
with our cat clawing to beat hell
in our compact,
not until I lay me down to dream
and the nightmares stop about moving
and the hills stop animating
under the stars like cartoons
and I stop taking personally
the laughter in the shrubbery
and the jocular wisdom about distinctions
between change and progress,
and then not until I step in class
and the clock stares into the unimaginable present
just a stroke or two past the middle
of my life, and not until
the newspaper boy rides by with
the rolled up morning news
and banks it perfectly on the porch
so I might know his name.

Shock Treatment

The other night I dreamed of the impulse
shuttling its way down a telephone wire
that would tell me something,
of my own death perhaps, and I woke
still dreaming, ran out of the house,
jumped in the car with only
my underwear on and drove
one maybe two blocks screaming,

trying to outrun something, or gain
whatever help I'd need,
and then I woke feeling shamed
and helpless. I've heard
the explanations: how the electrodes
placed on both temples
make memory expensive, how things
are safe now and that is bona fide
treatment. And I guess I am blessed,
having lived long enough in one town
to no longer dramatize in dreams
my moving or waking somewhere strange,

the floor askew, the walls a mass
of birdsong I hadn't listened to or
read about in the Field Guide.
And I am blessed says Steve Garvey on TV,

having gone four for four on a Sunday.

Coming Out

for Bob McGrath, neighbor

Yesterday at the T-Mart I saw
Junior's sister shaking hell
out of the gum machine in that
restless, vaguely pubescent way.
Ignore the Foo dog and it gets
bigger, right? More
than a dog ought to be.
More than basso-falsetto
on a passing afternoon.

Bob, she stood there shaking
then went off. She wondered
what might happen next—
what could? What else
in this odd machinery could
fail? And when has happiness
explained its own dark birth,
or sadness its borrowed nest?

The House for Sale across the Street

That house across the street is perfectly abandoned.
The door opens with a little nudge. So my cat and I
stalk it. The way his head jerks suddenly tells me
he's freely associating again, so fast I can't keep up with
any dignity.

The house is grazing now, staring straight ahead.
We are all three in a field. All in a green field
and one of us thinks he's human and two of us,
before we let ourselves back out, freeze in our own
likenesses to what we think is true.

I'm not going to tell you anything
about my own life. I'm not going to share a thing
with anyone present. Not about me. Not about me
when I was a boy.

Well, when I came home to supper late,
my father made me duckwalk around the living
room, full circle, a room about this size, average.
The thing is, I'd asked permission earlier,
and gotten it, from my mother, who had told my
                                        father, who
was drunk and insisted that I do it anyway because
he had to, when he was in the army.
And I don't care what you think. He was all right,
my father.

As people often say, my cat thinks
he's a person. When I let him out, he won't respond
to any call, even in the cold. I have to put on boots,
walk out past the drive, pitch my voice just so,
feel ashamed; then he's satisfied.
But he waits there, wherever he is, until he hears me say
it's all right. I miss you. Come home.

Part Two:
Windy Tuesday Nights

March 14–20, 1982, Year of the Eagle

—quoting a postage stamp

The claws of an eagle are called talons.
Well I know that but didn't know
I knew it. Some friends
sent a card and this information
on a stamp that framed a blue sky
and an eagle poised
above some snowy hills where, ordinarily,
at this time of year, a rabbit
would munch under the sun the cold
curly grass. *We care about eagles,*
the stamp said, and why not? *This is*
the year of the eagle, of caring
about it, of educating the general
dumb-ass public as to its claws,
which are talons, really.
You think I'm being terrible, don't you?
That two friends who send a card, a kind of
Forget-me-not mean, as we say, well.
Yes I know and I worry
about my not being kind. So
I go out and buy a card, this time a blank one,
and I draw the valentine that has haunted me
since childhood, using as model my
huge neighbor Beulah
as she bends in her orange pantsuit
to pick up some trash. The world around her
is clipped green, the air

so delicate and alive you
could bring the dead out
and have a picnic. Who would
want to? This is the year of the living.
The dog who licks his ass
is called Redbud. And so I lick
the back of a stamp, this time a picture of Babe Ruth,
King of Swat, who hit 60 home runs in 1927,
year of the 527-foot home run,
and I think, I'll smear
this on this envelope
and I think too, I'll send it.
And then I think who cares
what I think,
my friends remain my friends
and I am a long way away.

Testing the Current

Don't say, *Things happen
from time to time*—
they can't all happen all at once. Say, *That's
another story, and I don't want to talk about it.*
That spot at the base of my spine
that goes diagonally across my butt
has given me a hard time
for a long time.
I remember Old-What-Color-Is-It.
His greaser car was parked on a gravel drive
while we bounced a basketball on ours,
then held it, then God
knows why, threw it at
his newly painted car and said, *Hey,
what color is it this time?*
We had time to laugh. Of course
we thought him shabby, poor, before
he kicked us in our ass.
We said some angry things, indoors, at first,
I don't remember what, and then we wanted
to be friends.
We sent messages out with brothers, sisters, friends.
And thirty years from now he stands
glaring on the lawn,
a basketball, a knife, a sun raw red and turning blue.
He has all the time in the world.

The Big Money

I'm watching *Superman III* on my 19″ Sony Trinitron
which I bought along with other objects after receiving
money from the National Endowment for the Arts.
And a stereo, too, some Nike running shoes,
two new JBL speakers, and a Seiko watch.
And a boat, I have a boat out back, a bass boat.
I listen hard to the news, to hog futures and cash grains,
because the government can take it all back.
And I listen for static,
because you can get cheated. I remember once,
for two weeks, I saved lunch money to buy a gun,
because what if someone came up to me and
wanted my lunch money? Jimmy Olson is
hanging on to a building he can't hold on to
much longer. He once had a poem in *Poetry* magazine.
Later he became Jimmy Olson and now
he writes libretti for the big money.
I think we greedy ones must break
Superman's heart. I study the cape unfurled
like a flag of the commonwealth, his easy
offhand heroic stare, but wait . . . !
I bought a Pekinese. And he won't bark.
He lies and licks himself like any dog.
Like any old hound who eats and drinks
and sleeps under the Indian-giver sun
on any given day in the Metropolis.

The Subnormal Girl with a Cat

hangs on the fence, just up itself,
no longer asking names of the neighbors.

No, it is enough to solve rinds of red
melons pushed far into trash cans, or
the riddle of bone white sky cracked
by branch. It is enough to learn
the motor of one afternoon, one that
loves shoulders, neck, back, hair—

meanwhile, some of the neighbors
have spoken back, some have not.

The Jay

My wife says he simply flew before
he had to late at night. He'd flown
onto the porch and confused, flew into
this poem. Stared actually
at the pitch that dropped him
for a noisy star.

I've seen them in parks applauding
as a woman in a blue wig called
for her children. They say,
Be like us. Be like us. Refuse human ways.
What happens to them to keep them so amazed?
Every mark, every nimble line is a hard question.

They are bold in every sweet transgression.
They call you every name in the book.

Crocodiles

Have you heard
the one about the man who
got a hand caught
in a crocodile? Down at
the local bar he got trapped.
Help, help, my hand
has caught a crocodile.
And he shook. And his two
hands gathered us in.
The kind of thing you see
often in dreams. There's this
poor, high-strung man who wants to
curl up in a pocket and sleep
a drunken sleep. Well,
it's wrong to have a bruised hand
of nickels and dimes, and well,
it's bad to have a wounded hand
of knuckles with minds of their own.
There's this thin, liver-spotted man
who wants to forget the stones
he threw as a child, the stones
that sink in the dark moon
of the stream, the listening stones,
the dark stones of riddles and wounds.
Now, now,
just take it easy
cowboy.

Totsie

The neighbor's niece is marching outside
our window, unaware of herself. Some legends
have children marching off to war,
returning better than ever.
I play the album your Aunt Totsie
owned once, the Festival
of Marches. We forgot we had all these records.
In the nursing home, when she spoke,
she almost whispered, her white hair
long and matted, your mother incredulous,
Oh Totsie, you want beer?
You put lipstick and rouge on her
and I could tell you wanted to cry.
Yesterday the letter came that explained
why gas is so expensive. Now
the little girl has gone inside.
She must be doing what once
you must have done: Trying
on shoes and walking a little.
Making herself more lovely.
More even than Jesus.
More than the red girl with the white baton.

Yo

I'm not just in a brown recliner.
I'm in an old pickup truck.
My thick forefinger comes down.
Hello. This is my wave.
I don't know you
but we share a secret.
We know leaves fall.
We know how far down
a road we share a dead fact.
We are the bones
of a small bird
and we give him all
we have left. Hello.
Can you hear me?
All we have.

Windy Tuesday Nights

Wasn't there a dark-eyed moribund crow
who died on August and flew,
naturally superfluous?

In my solo way I'm drunk again,
returned to the *genius loci*
of the one piss-elm.

The mayor's mistress is alone tonight!
And a thousand stars lie buried
in my old Dodge! There's

a bottomless mind behind this universe!

Recidivist

The same pictures find her and leave her.
Like sons and daughters moved away
earth-colored birds sleep separately
in cages covered with cloth.

She is the last of the wild sisters,
the rooms they become, walls
they come to know. Tomorrow
the sun settles in small patches,

what circles above has circled above before.
In sprinklers, from all edges of
the lawn, neighbor children
come to dance.

Tonight she sees her son walking through one gate
then another.
She will wait for him
in every cell, imagining

the walls wash him
and let him go home,
where the sun is softer than
the days allow,

the same things happen,
they will happen again.

Part Three:
A Circling of Real Wind

Tall Tale

In Bradford Woods
just after larch
and catalpa, blue ash
and tupelo gum, like
an idea whose time returns,
a cougar sleeps, dreaming
us. He needs only return
to black ponds and everywhere
what sings in the dusk
seems to grow teeth.
A tedious rain replies:
it is only a lie,
these woods are too near
town, only a dream
told over like a life or
just a bold cat.

But soon a friend brings
a tale to start a tale,
a circling of real wind,
and the cougar starts up,
as of himself, as we do,
upsets leaves
and a little bark and back
in a town we cannot name
where old men wave
freely from porches, pitch
the moon like horseshoes,

none of this will ever change,
even when the air comes bright
and wet as day labor,
even as we sleep.

The Barrens of Washington County

See it on thick days they told me.
Prairie grass, undulating rock, these barrens
bring an imitated grief, preferred sun,
slow bend of meadow fern. We wonder
why we're here, these hills holding back.
Here I bring my cruel things: a father
I slapped once, a girl so ugly
I laughed while she rubbed red
in her eyes. And I have brought
this grief, this violin
that pulls and pulls
at this long silence
and these returning weeds.

Donkey

Even though I hate to run
I dream of running,
puffing along the dirty Ohio,
Ohio of despair.
The women I pass look out at the various debris
and I am filled with sexual longing.
I've been out of town so long.
And I think of how we need to hurt the river back,
run our hands through it, pick it up,
twist it. In that fair
I went to once in one of these places,
in that donkey basketball game
where the donkeys wore rubber shoes
and were prodded electrically by boys,
I tried to justify my need to feel superior,
as if a river couldn't drown me,
as if an action truly spoke louder
than a word.
I shouldn't have been there,
so near the river's despair
that the ponies had moss on their backs
like ponies of bright desire.

Dear Sue,

Do the rivers whistle when you go away
like children afraid of the dark?
Brambles lie out in this soup, smoke
makes friends with what's above
a fire. Every day you'd wake with one
more tick, complain your labor into
the same hard sun, you'd just jump
yourself into this white river
and swim out of your damn self.
But the rivers don't know where to
bill your backwash. Besides, they
probably agree with you:
They give back your loud hello.
Their dark spreads out like talk
in the Council Bluffs.

Auction

An owl muttered himself to sleep
in cottonwood. A mildewed mattress
went for two dollars, a vanity for ten.
Away from a show of hands, an old man
kept the moon locked in muzzy vision.
Lamplight boiled in the lip of his eye.
I sat on Naugahyde propped
by railroad ties. The old man spoke:

I only just turned eighty and
if you wonder why I don't look it
I'll tell you anyway it was the Lord.
Everyone and the moon locked
in vision. His boy standing by,
twelve and retarded. *But a nice boy.*
Wouldn't harm a thing. And never forgets.

And the old man veed his fingers: *When I was*
a young man, Satan was on this side, Jesus
on the other. He pointed to the valley:
And I was here. Now we all know
vee stands for victory and
we all want victory so
I had to get from here to here.

A lanternfly sang around the boy's head.
He emptied out his pockets: a chewing gum
wrapper, two Lifesavers, a crayon.
From under a baseball cap his clear
eyes said *Take. Eat.* And his face widened
to a bridge.

All heads turned to the antique clock
huddled in canvas wings.
And the hands they waved like wheat
and the slow voice of wheat. The old man
pocketed his watch and like a deer, the boy
walked all directions of a dream.

And rain leaned toward the wheat
and the people they bid for his shadow.

Catatonic

"The best surprise is death."
                    —Josephine Jacobsen

Her foot has gone to sleep.
Outside, the humid air is like the time
she had to be quiet in fourth grade to keep
from being hit. Not to stir is one thing,
but to will the whole body to sleep. . . .

When I sit still, having nothing to say,
like now, I think of those thousands
in any town or hospital who lay
themselves down or sprawl like the place
itself, like the grasses, bleached.

There's a railroad nearby, near the window,
and when a train passes, she sleeps,
she watches the Minnetonka glide through Minnesota,
where snow falls loose in a young girl's hair.

School Dream

You have on new clothes. Today
you meet your French teacher.
A short dog-eared woman with croutons
for breasts. You are eleven
but this doesn't alarm you.
The eccentricities of academia have passed
your way before. A girl in back
raises a hand even before class starts.
You know you've had it.
Assignments will rain like straw.
The girl's hair is matted
and she has obviously been picking her nose.
The question is abstract, loaded
with bad breath. The class roars.
You are relieved. All this time
you have been standing by
the pencil sharpener, pee
dripping from your new pants.
You are quiet about it.
You know another dream where the girl
is red and white, stepping from a hot bath.
You begin to crack a smile.

The One Who Stays Home

The plump girl in the dark green chair
can scarcely remember that state with
big trees. It might've been a place
where people stood, herself maybe, only
older, like the redwoods. Was it north?
Somewhere in the middle west?

Some say we proceed from what we forget
and our proportions change. So gladiolas
on a wall drift east like Iowa corn
or sing huge songs in the absence of Texas.
Opening her closet, pulling the long string
of the one bare bulb, the fat girl numbers

the robes of her own geography. If
they were more beautiful, she thinks,
if they only had wings. . . . Some nights
alone in her parents' house she trills
like an insect. Soon of course she's furious.
More hurt than anything, really.

Part Four:
The Shetland Islands

The Shetland Islands

She was so impressed with the Shetland Islands
she bought a pair of pony fur boots
and gave them on Christmas to her daughter.

He could still remember the snow
and the otters,
the magnificent grays
and the wind.

Some papers were spread on the table
where she had done the income tax.
And a photograph, too, of an otter,
two maybe, three,
an ottery tangle.

The males, the male ducks, he remembered,
were encouraged by the drab females.

He thought, all those animals
have lives that continue as before
and he thought, with a feeling of virtue,
we needed a vacation
and hell, we took one,
we just left.

He could almost understand the abandon
of the great explorers—
La Salle, the Admiral Byrd.

He washed the plates and one by one,
the knives and forks and spoons.
It's the way to be, he thought.
And then, as was usual
far into those nights,
he began to qualify.

Going somewhere is not so much.
But knowing when counts.

The Gift

for W. O. and Michael Heffernan

When my father-in-law gave me the knife,
a small pocketknife, enameled, one
his father gave to him, he said don't
lose it, it means we remain friends.
Years took a cynical turn: he and his wife
divorced, and he accused his daughter and me
of taking sides. The last time I saw the knife
I was cutting line at Jack Knoll's private pond.
I remember putting it down with the rest
of the tackle, I think, or on the ground,
to be honest, on the ground somewhere,
or is it around *here* somewhere,
in the crook of my arm, or yours, maybe,
or there, beneath the river grass, old friend,
maybe, possibly.

The Collection

Her friends lift them one by one
from case and mantelpiece, wishing:
I wish I had this one;
or: *Oh honey, here's one with a chip*
but it makes you and me happy.

Her friends delight in her elephants
and probably there's a kind of procession.

They raise their trunks, if they didn't,
people might put them right back down.

They crouch all night waiting to be elected.

And Noah himself would search the cities and towns
listening for that right, crude, nasal song
on those thick, yellow, glass shelves at five-and-dimes.
While the rest of us wept in imitation.

48

December Twentieth

A cold morning in December, five days
before the shit flies. The rage
of people who should be happy and know it.
The pipes below the bathtub are frozen

and now the hairdrier I use for thawing
throws its voice: It's sad.
The way things speed up and slow down.
To borrow a line: *Life is sad.*
                              And further,

death too, death is sad. Ella might be singing now,
not quite in this world, not out,
but the radio's busted.
So I listen all morning

for the phone, and not a word.
I never know when you are angry,

never sense you are hurt, crazy, or alone.

Remembering My Father

How it was I guess
in this familiar room
all morning, into next
week—a few stubble fields that
catch the moon, him cursing,
or cussing like we really said,
him cussing under whiskey breath,
driving or letting me drive
on his lap, his tan
calfskin jacket
over us both, my legs and feet mostly
because even though it's June it's cold.
More than once he'd slap me into driving
down the straight and the narrow.
I scared him damn it, the way
I drove. The father
I thought he was watches
the son I think I am
who hears only the noise
a finger leaves on this picture window.
What holds our image in
and yours needs no explanation.
Only a reason for driving
those night roads, him
letting me steer, me with so
much straight and narrow.
And this constant return
or lack of return
to this scene with a moon so far away it's urban,

to the lake we left ten, maybe twenty, miles back
with a stringer of fish I accidentally dropped there.
The child at the picture window
thinks I'm trying to remember
that lake, the stringer he let go of,
the whole red night,
but I'm not. They can all go swim with the fish.
I have forgotten the ways
the father calms the son, tries to calm them both
as they look in those waters
for that strange family
that swims somehow together.